The Women of the
U.S. Supreme Court

Growing Up Supremely

by Jessica L. Armstrong
& Nichola D. Gutgold

Illustrated by
Delilah Jabbour

Eifrig Publishing LLC

Berlin Lemont

© 2024 Jessica L. Armstrong & Nichola D. Gutgold
Printed in the United States of America

All rights reserved. This publication is protected by Copyright, and permission should be obtained from the publisher prior to any prohibited reproduction, storage in a retrieval system, or transmission in any form or by any means, electronic, mechanical, photocopying, recording, or likewise.

Published by Eifrig Publishing,
PO Box 66, Lemont, PA 16851, USA
Knobelsdorffstr. 44, 14059 Berlin, Germany.

For information regarding permission, write to:
Rights and Permissions Department,
Eifrig Publishing,
PO Box 66, Lemont, PA 16851, USA.
permissions@eifrigpublishing.com, +1 814 954 9445

Library of Congress Cataloging-in-Publication Data
Armstrong, Jessica & Nichola D. Gutgold

Growing Up Supremely: The Women of the U.S. Supreme Court /
by Jessica L. Armstrong & Nichola D. Gutgold, illustrated by Delilah Jabbour
p. cm.

Paperback: ISBN 978-1-63233-357-5
Hard cover: ISBN 978-1-63233-358-2
eBook: ISBN 978-1-63233-359-9

[1. Biography/Women - Juvenile Non-Fiction. 2. U.S. Supreme Court - Juvenile Non-Fiction.]

I. Jabbour, Delilah, ill. II. Title

27 26 25 24 2023
5 4 3

Printed on recycled acid-free paper. ∞

~When **Sandra Day O'Connor** was growing up, she lived many miles away from any other kids.

~**Ruth Bader Ginsburg**'s mom died when she was just a teenager.

~**Sonia Sotomayor** was diagnosed with Type 1 Diabetes at age seven and began taking daily insulin injections. Her father died when she was only nine years old.

~**Elena Kagan** grew up as the middle child and questioned her family's religious rituals.

~**Amy Coney Barrett** grew up the oldest of seven children in New Orleans, Louisiana. She was often put in charge of her young siblings, even at an early age.

~**Ketanji Brown Jackson** was born in Washington, DC, and her name, Ketanji, is African and means "lovely one." She was often made to feel like she didn't belong or wasn't good enough because she was Black and female.

While they each grew up in different environments and faced different challenges and circumstances,

they do have one major thing in common:

They all grew up to become ... Supreme Court Justices!

What is the Supreme Court?

The United States **Supreme Court** is the highest court in the land, and it is located in Washington, D.C., the nation's capital. The Supreme Court decides the laws of the United States. It was started in 1789, but it took almost two hundred years before the first woman was appointed as a Supreme Court Justice. Since that time, only six women have served on the Supreme Court, while over 100 men have served. The court consists of nine justices, who can stay on the court as long as they want. It is not easy to become a Supreme Court Justice. The President of the United States must nominate you, and then you must get the okay (known as the **confirmation**) from the Senate.

What do the Justices do?

Like other judges, Supreme Court Justices listen to civil and criminal cases. However, the Justices get to choose which cases to hear. Only about 100 cases a year are heard by the Supreme Court, but these are the most important ones in the land. The Justices are responsible for explaining and interpreting the **Constitution** and they interpret laws passed by Congress. All of the other courts in the land must follow the rulings of the Supreme Court.

What type of cases are decided?

Often the cases are about basic civil rights and freedoms that are protected by the **Bill of Rights**. The Supreme Court has decided cases about public school desegregation (Brown v. Board of Education), the right to privacy to protect a woman's right of choice (Roe v. Wade), the right to an attorney even if you cannot afford one (Gideon v. Wainright), prisoners must be advised of their rights before being questioned by police (Miranda v. Arizona), the right of school children to freedom of expression (Tinker v. Des Moines)

The justices will read briefs, listen to oral arguments and then go into conference. The justices may not agree with each other, but the majority rules. Many decisions end up with the judges voting 5 to 4. Once the justices have voted, one person is chosen to write a **majority opinion**. If some of the justices disagree, they can write a **dissent**.

Sandra Day O'Connor | Ruth Bader Ginsburg | Sonia Sotomayor

Elena Kagan | Amy Coney Barrett | Ketanji Brown Jackson

Who are the first six women of the US Supreme Court?

Sandra Day O'Connor

Ruth Bader Ginsburg

Sonia Sotomayor

Elena Kagan

Amy Coney Barrett

Ketanji Brown Jackson

Sandra Day O'Connor (1981~2006)

Sandra was born in Texas and grew up on a cattle ranch in Arizona. It was far away from any other place and had no running water or electricity until she was seven years old. Just think of a day without running water! How would you brush your teeth or wash your hands? But Sandra and her family were resourceful and strong. She hunted from a young age, using a rifle to shoot jackrabbits for food. Without any children her age nearby and when not helping out around the farm, Sandra would sit under a large tree and read. Books were her favorite gift. Because her family's ranch was so far from schools, for most of her young life Sandra lived with her grandmother where she attended an all-girls school. When she was in eighth grade, however, she returned to the ranch and took a school bus 32 miles each way to school.

Sandra loved to learn and graduated top in her class in high school. She then headed to Stanford University in California. She graduated from Stanford and earned a law degree from there, as well. In law school she met her future husband, John O'Connor. Even though she had a great education, Sandra could not find a job when she graduated law school~because she was a woman. At that time, there were hardly any female **lawyers** and many law firms would not hire a woman as a lawyer.

Sandra Day O'Connor eventually found a job as an **attorney** after she offered to work for no salary and without an office, sharing space with a secretary. When her husband was drafted, she decided to go with him to work in Germany as an attorney for the Army's Quartermaster Corps. They remained there for three years before returning to the States where they settled in Arizona. They had three sons, and Sandra volunteered for various political organizations and served as assistant Attorney General of Arizona before going on to fill a seat in the Arizona Senate. She became the first woman to serve as Arizona's or any state's Majority Leader. She became known as a skilled negotiator.

She was elected to the Superior Court and then was elevated to the Arizona State Court of Appeals. She served on the Court of Appeals until she was appointed to the Supreme Court by President Ronald Reagan. She was the first woman in the United States to serve on the Supreme Court.

How do you think being raised on a ranch may have helped Sandra overcome challenges she faced throughout her career?

Ruth was sometimes asked when will there be enough women on the Supreme Court, and she answered, "When there are nine." There had been nine men on the court for a long time, and nobody ever raised a question about that.

Ruth Bader Ginsburg (1993 ~ 2020)

Ruth Joan Bader was born in Brooklyn, NY, and from a very young age she loved to read and write. In grade school, she wrote for the student newspaper and learned about the **Magna Carta**, a document that described rights and freedoms. Her mother encouraged her to keep learning and was a role model to young Ruth. Sadly, Ruth's mom died just before Ruth graduated from high school. Although she was very sad to lose one of her biggest supporters, Ruth persisted and attended Cornell University, where she graduated with high honors in government. She then married Martin Ginsburg, a law student.

What do you think Ruth's early experiences may have taught her about discrimination?

She went on to Harvard Law School where she served on the Law Review. In the male-dominated world of law, Ruth Bader Ginsburg was told that she and her eight female classmates—out of a class of five-hundred—were taking the places of qualified men. This kind of discrimination reminded her of growing up in Brooklyn, where she and her family were often excluded because they were Jewish. Ruth wanted to fight against unfairness. She transferred to Columbia University after two years when her husband took a job in New York. Although she graduated at the top of her class, law firms refused to hire her. Despite this challenging start, she went on to become a courtroom advocate for the fair treatment of women and worked with the American Civil Liberty Union's (ACLU) Women's Rights Project.

Ruth Bader Ginsburg was appointed by President Carter to the U.S. Court of Appeals in 1980 and was appointed to the Supreme Court by President Clinton in 1993. She paid tribute to her mother in her speech in the Rose Garden of the White House when she said:

"I have a last thank you. It is to my mother, Celia Amster Bader, the bravest, strongest person I have known, who was taken from me much too soon," she said in a slow, measured voice. "I pray that I may be all that she would have been, had she lived in an age when women could aspire and achieve, and daughters are cherished as much as sons."

Sonia Sotomayor (2009 ~ today)

Sonia Sotomayor was born in the South Bronx area of New York City to parents of Puerto Rican descent. Her mother was a nurse, and her father was a factory worker. Young Sonia loved to watch Perry Mason, a television show about a lawyer. She noticed that the judge on the TV show got to make the big decisions, and she thought that is what she'd like to do. She also loved reading Nancy Drew mysteries.

When her father died, Sonia was still a young girl, and her mom worked hard to raise Sonia and her brother as a single parent. She placed a lot of emphasis on a higher education, pushing her children to become fluent in English and making huge sacrifices to purchase a set of encyclopedias that would give them proper research materials for school. Sonia graduated from high school in the Bronx and entered Princeton University. She was overwhelmed by her new school; after she received low marks on first mid-term paper, she sought help from a professor, and she challenged herself by taking more English and writing classes. She also became a leader with the Puerto Rican groups on campus and worked with the university's **discipline** committee, where she started developing her legal skills.

How do you think Sonia's determination to do well in school may have made a difference in her future?

All of Sonia's hard work paid off when she graduated **summa cum laude** from Princeton. That same year, she entered Yale Law School, where she was an editor for the Yale Law Journal. After she graduated Yale Law School, she began work as an **assistant district attorney** in New York City.

Sonia was responsible for prosecuting robbery, assault, murder, and police brutality cases. Later she entered private practice. She also worked for free at non-profit agencies.

She was appointed as U.S. District Court judge and became a judge for the U.S. Second Circuit Court of Appeals. In 2009, President Barack Obama announced his nomination of Sonia Sotomayor for Supreme Court justice. Sonia became the first Latina Supreme Court justice in U.S. history.

Elena Kagan (2010 ~ today)

Born in New York City, Elena Kagan grew up as the second of three children in a middle-class Jewish family living on Manhattan's Upper West Side. Elena's mother was an educator, teaching students at Hunter College Elementary School. Her father was a lawyer at a Manhattan law firm, where he worked primarily to help tenants fight for their rights against landlords. Inspired by her father's work, Elena took an interest in law at an early age.

Also influenced by her mother's strong beliefs in getting a good education, Elena attended an all-girls school. She felt comfortable being a smart girl in this school, surrounded by other girls. After she graduated from high school, she went to Princeton University, where she studied history and graduated in 1981 **summa cum laude** with a Bachelor's degree. She also earned a scholarship from Princeton, which allowed her to attend Worcester College in Oxford, England.

She earned a Master's degree in Philosophy at Worcester before moving on immediately to Harvard Law School, where she became supervising editor of the Harvard Law Review and graduated **magna cum laude**.

When she was a little girl, Elena loved working hard in school. How do you think that may have helped her later in life?

After law school, Elena **clerked** for two different justices. The next year, she began another clerking job for Justice Thurgood Marshall of the U.S. Supreme Court. During this time, she also worked on a political campaign, but then returned to **academia**—as a professor. In 1991, she began teaching at the University of Chicago Law School, and by 1995, she was a tenured professor of law. Elena left the school that same year, however, to work as a lawyer for President Bill Clinton.

During her years at the White House, Elena was promoted many times, because she worked hard and used her intelligence. She started as a visiting professor at Harvard Law and then was named **dean** of Harvard Law School. After fellow Harvard alumnus Barack Obama won the 2008 presidential election, he selected Elena for the role of **Solicitor General**.

With her confirmation, she became the first woman to serve as Solicitor General of the United States. Just two months after her confirmation as Solicitor General, President Obama nominated Kagan the Supreme Court, and she became the fourth woman to sit on the high court. In addition, her approval put three female justices—Kagan, Ruth Bader Ginsburg and Sonia Sotomayor—on the country's highest court for the first time in U.S. history.

Amy Coney Barrett (2020 ~ today)

Amy grew up in a devoutly Catholic home where her parents emphasized education and religion. A natural born leader, Amy was vice-president of her all-girls Catholic high school senior class and a role model to her six younger siblings and classmates who admired her service to her school and her careful attention to her studies.

After high school, Amy attended Rhodes College, where she majored in English literature and minored in French. She graduated in with a Bachelor of Arts magna cum laude and was inducted into Omicron Delta Kappa and Phi Beta Kappa, both prestigious honor societies. In her graduating class, she was named most outstanding English department graduate.

Barrett then attended the Notre Dame Law School on a full-tuition scholarship. She was recognized as the top student in her graduating class. Like other justices, Amy worked as a law clerk for other justices. She also worked in law firms and taught at law schools, and finally worked as a judge for the Court of Appeals.

Ketanji Brown Jackson (2022 ~ today)

Ketanji and her family moved from Washington, DC to Miami, Florida so her dad could attend law school. She would see her dad's law books piled high, and she would stack her coloring books up in a high pile to mimic the look of her dad's law books. Her mother, a school principal, emphasized academics and encouraged Ketanji to excel.

In high school she won a national public speaking contest, was a speech and debate team star, and aspired to be a judge.

Even if other people sometimes underestimated Ketanji, she believed in herself and wanted to show them she could achieve her highest goals. She went on to study government at Harvard University and attended Harvard Law School.

After graduating from law school, she clerked for justices and worked as a public defender. She faced discrimination as a Black woman, but found that choosing a middle ground to bring people together was a powerful way to overcome obstacles.

What do these six women have in common?

They all worked very hard to get a good education.

They all overcame tough obstacles in life.

They were not afraid to try new things and to be the first to do something.

They each spoke up and spoke well!

All of the women loved to read from the time they were little girls.

Do you like to read? If so, you can grow up supremely too!

Can you think of some other things that these women have in common?

What are some of the firsts that these women achieved?

First female Supreme Court Justice: Sandra Day O'Connor

First female Jewish Supreme Court Justice: Ruth Bader Ginsberg

First Hispanic Supreme Court Justice: Sonia Sotomayor

First Black female Supreme Court Justice: Ketanji Brown Jackson

Motto of the Supreme Court: *Equal Justice Under Law*

Glossary

- **academia** ~ an environment or community concerned with the pursuit of research, education and scholarship
- **assistant district attorney** ~ a law enforcement official who represents the state government on behalf of the district attorney in investigating and prosecuting individuals alleged to have committed a crime
- **attorney** ~ one who advises or represents others in legal matters as a profession
- **Bill of Rights** ~ the first ten amendments to the US Constitution, ratified in 1791
- **clerked** ~ a law student is said to have "clerked" when she or he assists a judge with the preparation of legal cases
- **confirmation** ~ the constitutional requirement that nominations to the U.S. Supreme Court be approved by the Senate
- **conviction** ~ a firmly held belief or opinion
- **dean** ~ A dean is the head of a specific area of a college, university, or private school
- **dissent** ~ an explicit disagreement by one or more judges with the decision of the majority on a case before them
- **lawyer** ~ a person who practices or studies law; an attorney or a counselor (see also attorney, above)
- **majority opinion** ~ a decision of the court agreed to by more than half the justices
- **Magna Carta** ~ a document constituting a fundamental guarantee of rights and privileges
- **magna cum laude** ~ an honor awarded to high-achieving students at colleges, just below summa cum laude (see below)
- **professor** ~ a teacher of the highest rank in a college or university
- **Solicitor General** ~ the law officer directly below the Attorney General in the U.S. Department of Justice, responsible for arguing cases before the U.S. Supreme Court
- **summa cum laude** ~ an honor awarded to students who have graduated from college with the highest grades
- **Supreme Court** ~ the highest judicial court in a country or state

Quotes from the Women

Justice Sandra Day O'Connor
102nd Justice (1981-2006)

"Society as a whole, benefits immeasurably from a climate in which all persons, regardless of race or gender, may have the opportunity to earn respect, responsibility, advancement and remuneration based on ability."

"I think the important thing about my appointment is not that I will decide cases as a woman, but that I am a woman who will get to decide cases."

Justice Ruth Bader Ginsburg
107th Justice (1993-2020)

"Women will only have true equality when men share with them the responsibility of bringing up the next generation."

"What has become of me could happen only in America. Like so many others, I owe so much to the entry this nation afforded to people yearning to breathe free."

Justice Sonia Sotomayor
111th Justice (2009-present)

"Until we get equality in education, we won't have an equal society."

"It is important for all of us to appreciate where we come from and how that history has really shaped us in ways that we might not understand."

on the Supreme Court

Justice Elena Kagan
112th Justice (2010-present)

"Law matters because it keeps us safe, because it protects our most fundamental rights and freedoms, and because it is the foundation of our democracy."

"It was a very cool thing to be a smart girl, as opposed to some other, different kind. And I think that made a great deal of difference to me growing up and in my life afterward."

Justice Amy Coney Barrett
115th Justice (2020-present)

"It is never appropriate for a judge to apply their personal convictions, whether it derives from faith or personal conviction."

Justice Ketanji Brown Jackson
116th Justice (2022-present)

"You can't always expect to be the smartest person in the room, but you can promise to be the hardest working."

"It has taken 232 years and 115 prior appointments for a Black woman to be selected to serve on the Supreme Court of the United States, but we've made it! We've made it — all of us."

"Our children are telling me that they see now, more than ever, that, here in America, anything is possible."

About the Authors

Jessica L. Armstrong is a mother, a lawyer, an activist, and a reader. She knew she wanted to be a lawyer from a young age, when she discovered the joys of reading, writing and speaking. Jessica holds a BA in American Studies from Stanford University and a JD from University of San Francisco. Today she works as a healthcare attorney for a regional non-profit healthcare organization. She reveres the Constitution and is thrilled to be involved with introducing children to the women of the Supreme Court.

Nichola D. Gutgold is a mother, a wife, and a professor of communication arts and sciences who has authored over ten books and several children's books that amplify the voices of women. She enjoys extending the lessons of extraordinary women to young people who may shape their own lives with the inspirational stories of real, ordinary women who accomplished extraordinary things.

About the Illustrator

Delilah Jabbour is a student at Penn State Abington following an Integrative Arts degree with a focus on Fine Arts and Museum Studies. This is her first time illustrating a book, and she enjoys placing narratives into her art. She plans to earn an MFA in Museum Exhibition & Design and dedicate her career to raising awareness through art, whether it is through her own work or curating exhibitions.

www.ingramcontent.com/pod-product-compliance
Lightning Source LLC
Chambersburg PA
CBHW040011080526
44586CB00028B/2963